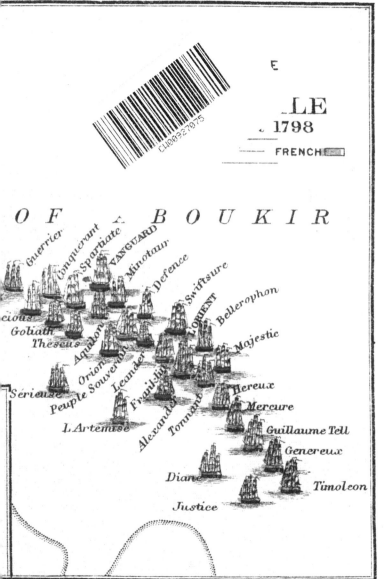

E

LE
1798

FRENCH

O F — BOUKIR

Guerrier
Conquerant
Spartiate
VANGUARD
Minotaur
Defence
Swiftsure
cious
Goliath
LORIENT
Bellerophon
Theseus
Aquilon
Majestic
Orion
Serieuse
Peuple Souverain
Leander
Franklin
Hereux
L.Artemise
Alexander
Mercure
Tonnant
Guillaume Tell
Genereux
Diane
Timoleon
Justice

F.S.Weller.F.R.G.S.

Series 117

This is a Ladybird Expert book, one of a series of titles for an adult readership. Written by some of the leading lights and outstanding communicators in their fields and published by one of the most trusted and well-loved names in books, the Ladybird Expert series provides clear, accessible and authoritative introductions, informed by expert opinion, to key subjects drawn from science, history and culture.

The publisher wishes to thank the following for the illustrative references for this book:
Shutterstock. Endpaper map from a school atlas of English history by Samuel Rawson Gardiner, 1829, from archive.com.

Every effort has been made to ensure images are correctly attributed, however if any omission or error has been made please notify the Publisher for correction in future editions.

MICHAEL JOSEPH

UK | USA | Canada | Ireland | Australia
India | New Zealand | South Africa

Michael Joseph is part of the Penguin Random House group of companies
whose addresses can be found at global.penguinrandomhouse.com

 Penguin
Random House
UK

First published 2019
001

A CIP catalogue record for this book is available from the British Library
ISBN: 978-0-718-18858-0

www.greenpenguin.co.uk

The Battle of the Nile

Sam Willis

with illustrations by
Paul Young

Ladybird Books Ltd, London

In February 1797 a thirty-eight-year-old British naval officer, Commodore Horatio Nelson, landed with fanfare, lights and fireworks on the public stage. He had just taken part in a naval battle against the Spanish, then allies of Revolutionary France, off Cape St Vincent. In that battle he had performed exceptionally; in fact, his performance was then, and still is, unique in British naval history.

From his two-decked 74-gun ship he had beaten a much larger 80-gunner into submission, boarded her at the head of his men and personally secured her captain's surrender. It was the first time that a British flag-officer had led a boarding party in person since Sir Edward Howard in 1513. From that ship he had then boarded a three-decked Spanish ship, this one of 112 guns, and had again personally secured her captain's surrender. The manoeuvre became known in the fleet as 'Nelson's Patent Bridge for Boarding First Rates'.

Shortly after his return to England, he was knighted, promoted to rear-admiral and his fame spread. This was some rise for the son of a vicar from rural Norfolk, but he wasn't about to stop there.

In less than a year his status had changed again, this time to National Hero. In the summer of 1798 he was given a peerage by King George III and a dukedom in Sicily by the King of Naples, which came with a 35,000 acre estate, a castle and a twelfth-century abbey; he took as his lover Emma Hamilton, one of the most famous women of the era; and received personal gifts from the Tsar of Russia and the Sultan of the Ottoman Empire.

The catalyst for this remarkable transformation was the Battle of the Nile of 1–3 August 1798, one of the most important battles that has ever been fought on land or sea.

The roots of the battle lie in the French Revolution. In 1793, five years before the Battle of the Nile, the French executed their king, Louis XVI. He was beheaded by a guillotine in a public square in the centre of Paris. He did not die as a king but as a citizen; as *citoyen* Louis Capet. Every one of his final requests was denied.

The effect of this regicide was immense and immediate. The Capetian monarchy had been founded in AD 987 and Capetian kings had reigned uninterrupted for a total of 806 years: there are few more profound schisms in history than this moment, when the orthodox, expected and understood were swept away for a new, and as yet unknown, order.

After Louis's murder, France was threatened on all sides as traditional European states including Austria, the Holy Roman Empire, Prussia, England, Spain, the Dutch Republic, Portugal, Sardinia, Tuscany and Naples reacted in horror to the regicide and took up arms against her, initially with great success.

The Austrians invaded northern France; the British took French possessions in the West Indies and the port of Toulon in southern France; the Sardinians crossed the Alps and the Spanish the Pyrenees; French possessions in the East Indies fell like dominoes.

In 1794, however, the French began to turn the tables on their enemies. Between April 1793 and July 1794, a period which became known as the 'Reign of Terror', a politician named Maximilien Robespierre attempted to bring a chaotic Revolutionary France to heel through intimidation and fear.

During this period almost 17,000 people were officially sentenced to death and executed by guillotine; perhaps 40,000 more were executed without any record being kept, and 500,000 men and women were imprisoned for political crimes. Those who were not murdered or imprisoned were conscripted for the war effort.

In June 1794 the French took Belgium and the Rhineland and marched on the Netherlands. In January 1795 they took Amsterdam and completed their conquest of the Dutch Republic. From then until 1806 the Dutch, in the guise of the revolutionary-inspired 'Batavian Republic', were reluctant allies of the French.

In the summer of 1794 the French also invaded Spain and tasted overwhelming success against the combined armies of the kingdoms of Spain and Portugal. With thousands of French troops encamped on Spanish soil, the Spanish suddenly found it easier to remember their old alliances with France and in August they swapped sides, joining the French. The French and Spanish would remain allies until 1808.

As the Revolution tasted success and grew confident once more, Robespierre himself fell to the guillotine's blade when his cronies turned against his tyranny in June 1794. Thereafter France was governed by the Directory, a committee of five 'directors' committed to preventing too much power from residing in the hands of one man: first it had been Louis the king and then Robespierre the politician. They were determined that it would not happen yet again.

One of the Directory's leading generals, however, was a Corsican from a minor branch of the nobility called Napoleon Bonaparte. Napoleon had excelled as a soldier in the early years of the Revolution. In October 1795 he had demonstrated his loyalty to the new post-Robespierre regime by putting down a coup intended to reinstate the monarchy.

In the spring of 1796 he was given command of the army in Italy. Although he lacked resources and was badly outnumbered, Napoleon immediately won territory for France and left his enemy's armies in pieces.

First, in north-west Italy, he defeated the Austrians and Sardinians, captured the country of Piedmont and forced Sardinia out of the war. Then, in a series of battles, he drove the Austrians out of Italy and chased them to within a hundred miles of Vienna. In the process of that advance he also captured the Republic of Venice, ending eleven hundred years of its independence as a city-state.

It was only at sea that the Revolution was checked. The French painted their ships red for the blood that ran in the streets and flew silk banners from their ships proclaiming '*Marins La République Ou La Mort*' – 'Sailors The Republic or Death' – but they were no match for the British.

The French navy was purged during the Revolution. Hundreds of experienced but aristocratic officers were imprisoned, executed or forced to flee. They were replaced by men who were skilled sailors, but a significant vacuum in leadership and experience of command still existed, and in battle it showed. In June 1794 the revolutionaries suffered a major defeat to the British in the mid-Atlantic, in a battle which became known as the Glorious First of June.

France's allied naval powers, Spain and the Batavian Republic, were also comparatively weak in battle when confronted with the Royal Navy's strong ships and powerful guns manned by their well-trained and resourceful men. In February 1797 the Spanish were defeated at the Battle of Cape St Vincent when Nelson first won his fame, and in October that year the navy of the Batavian Republic was defeated at the Battle of Camperdown.

In spite of these defeats, however, the French navy remained a significant strategic force, particularly in its ability to transport troops to distant, vulnerable and unexpected locations.

After his victory in Italy, Napoleon had become increasingly influential in politics in France and had further cemented his position by providing military assistance to a coup d'état in September 1797 which had seized power from a branch of the Directory with royalist sympathies. A month later he signed the Treaty of Campo Formio, which officially ended Austria's involvement in the war against France. France's only remaining enemy was Great Britain and Napoleon became a national hero.

In 1798 Napoleon's ambitious eye fell on Egypt, a province of the Ottoman Empire but under the control of the Mameluks, who had ruled Egypt for centuries. Napoleon didn't just see Egypt as valuable territory but as a way of weakening the British Empire by cutting off its quickest route to British possessions in India. It would also provide a location from which the French could launch an attack on India itself: for Napoleon, Egypt was the key to an entire new overseas empire.

The Directory liked his thinking, and, in this era of scheming, faction and coups, they also liked the idea of this ambitious general being sent as far away from Paris as possible. Whispers of Napoleon's potential to become a dictator, meanwhile, grew louder.

Many British sailors had won their laurels of glory in these early years of the French Revolutionary Wars, but none more so than Horatio Nelson, and in spring 1798 he was given command of a detached squadron of the Mediterranean Fleet, the jewel in the Royal Navy's crown.

The Mediterranean was a crucial command because it was a key source of valuable British trade and it was also full of enemy ships. In August 1796 the Spanish had allied with the French, bringing the size of their combined fleet to 132 ships of the line, significantly larger than the Royal Navy's 123.

The Royal Navy's Mediterranean Fleet was one of the best in the age of sail, the unusual quality the result of a unique mixture of excellent ships and excellent men.

One of the problems of warfare under sail was the varied performance and size of individual ships, but Nelson's new squadron consisted almost entirely of two-decked 74-gunners, more than half of which had been built in the 1780s within a single year of each other. These ships were a perfect compromise between speed and power, a hunting squadron capable of facing the largest of enemies, the monstrous three-decked Spanish and French warships.

To hold their own against such enemies, however, Nelson's captains would have to act together with little guidance and his crews act skilfully with little rest.

In preparation for just such an engagement, Nelson drilled his crews daily in gunnery, which required teamwork and skill to a level of artistry for a ship to realize its potential as a weapon of war.

Under sail, a ship pitched, rolled, yawed, rose and fell as the waves passed underneath, every movement significantly affecting the positioning of both the firing ship and its target. Before a round was fired the gun had to be cleaned, primed, loaded with a cartridge, a ball and a wad, and then physically manoeuvred into the required position. The heaviest guns were the weight of a small car. No fewer than eight men and as many as twelve performed this intricate but heavyweight dance every time a gun was fired.

Nelson also made certain that his captains were all familiar with his tactical ideas to minimize the need for signalling in battle. Such was the chaos of naval warfare, such was the dense cloud of smoke raised by the hundreds – and sometimes thousands – of cannon, that no fleet could be controlled by an admiral as puppet-master.

His captains responded well. Nelson later described them as 'the finest Squadron that ever graced the Ocean'.

To get his army to Egypt, Napoleon needed a large fleet, which he amassed at the French naval base at Toulon. The size of the fleet is astonishing. It was over three times the size of the Spanish Armada of 1588. Forty thousand soldiers and ten thousand sailors had been raised and distributed amongst thirteen ships of the line, fourteen frigates and three hundred troop transports.

It was manned by some of the finest fighting men of the age. Among those on board, apart from Napoleon himself, were Louis-Alexandre Berthier, August de Marmont, Jean Lannes, Joachim Murat, Louis Desaix, Jean Reynier, Antoine-François Andréossy, Jean-Andoche Junot, Louis-Nicolas Davout and Alexandre Dumas – the core of the generals and marshals who, in the coming years, expanded and defended Napoleon's empire.

From observing Toulon, Nelson and his captains knew that a naval operation of great significance was imminent, but they had no idea what it entailed. Such ignorance of the enemy's intentions was common in this period.

Britain had been under threat of invasion for several years and although a direct invasion of England now seemed unlikely, a landing in Wales or Ireland was certainly conceivable. Egypt was considered as a possible destination, but it was only one of several.

Nelson's squadron, therefore, although brimming with ability and confidence, was also beset by paralysis and uncertainty.

Napoleon's fleet consisted not only of soldiers and sailors but also of a large body of civilians whose presence made it unique.

Napoleon's plans for Egypt were not purely military. His confidence of victory was such that he took with him the population he would require to found a French colony and a body of scholars to study the Egyptian cradle of civilization. His was a long-term and grandiose plan both to expand the French empire and increase the store of human knowledge.

Mathematicians, astronomers, engineers, naturalists, geographers, chemists, architects and artists all crammed aboard the French fleet. With no room on the troop transports, these civilians sailed aboard Napoleon's warships, complete with all the equipment and material required to support an army, found a colony and study the world around them.

To gather so many diverse people and their equipment together, to get them on board and feed and water them, was an impressive logistical achievement, but it made his fleet extremely vulnerable.

A small British squadron held its position off Toulon, waiting for the French to make their move, but no blockade was ever watertight. The ships in harbour were safe from the elements but the blockading fleet was always at the mercy of the weather. Proximity to shore was always dangerous in square-rigged ships with their bluff hulls that were unable to make significant ground towards the wind.

When a storm rose on 21 May, therefore, Nelson's captains took the only available option – they sailed out to sea, away from the rocky coast and into the storm. The subsequent twenty-four hours were terrifying. Men died; Nelson's ship, HMS *Vanguard*, was dismasted and one of her anchors had to be cut away to prevent it from repeatedly smashing into the side of the ship. She had to be taken in tow for twenty hours.

When the storm died down and Nelson's ship, remarkably the only one with serious damage, had been ingeniously repaired with timber taken from throughout the squadron, he led his ships back to Toulon, where he was met with reinforcements. At Toulon, however, he found the harbour empty. The enormous French fleet had simply vanished.

Nelson headed south-east towards Naples where he hoped to pick up intelligence from the British envoy, Sir William Hamilton, but Napoleon had seized the rare opportunity for projecting threat that his great fleet offered and had sailed south to Malta, the fortified island home of the ancient Knights of St John. The Knights, who had withstood one of the greatest sieges in history against an Ottoman horde in 1565, were now a shadow of their former selves and offered but token resistance to the French.

The subsequent, though brief, French occupation brought a great deal of good to an island that had been stuck in time, not least the liberation of 2,000 slaves kept by the Knights as well as reforms which improved government administration, schools, hospitals and freedom of speech. Napoleon also, however, emptied the Knights' store of gold, jewels, statues and art amassed through centuries of fighting in the name of Christendom.

On 12 June Napoleon and his fleet left for Egypt and he planned to treat the Egyptians in exactly the same way as he had treated the Maltese: he would conquer them, steal their treasure and bring reform.

Nelson, meanwhile, had been hunting ceaselessly, but, unlike an army marauding through a country, leaving boot, cart and hoof marks, stripping villages of food and filling memories with astonishment, a fleet at sea left only the faintest of traces. In this situation, an admiral would send forth a starburst of frigates to find the scent and hunt it. They would scan the horizon, interrogate fisherman and merchantmen, signal to each other in a chain over vast distance, but here was the key weakness of the British fleet and Nelson felt it like a wound: 'My distress from want of frigates is extreme', he wrote.

Nelson was always one step behind. While the French were on their way to Malta, he was a little east of Toulon; while they were in Malta, he was off Naples; it was only when the French actually sailed to Egypt that the likelihood of their paths crossing actually arose.

On 21 June the lean British battle fleet came within snatching distance of the French leviathan, all slowed and encumbered with children, philosophers and treasure, and bearing the finest French officers who would carve up Europe in years to come.

The French knew how close they were to disaster and could hear the British signal guns, but the British saw and heard nothing, blinded by a curtain of mist.

Nelson, meanwhile, had acquired intelligence that Napoleon's destination was Alexandria. Again the fate of Europe hung on a spider's silk because, if he were to catch the vulnerable French fleet in the act of unloading its troops and stores, defeat would be certain.

Napoleon, however, spooked by the close encounter in the mist, had headed north towards Crete and slowed his course. When Nelson arrived in Alexandria, therefore, he was a day too early and left, frustrated, to search elsewhere. The French fleet arrived at Alexandria on 1 July and disembarked entirely unopposed but in total chaos, their unity torn apart by wind and wave.

Within a few days, in the shadow of the Great Pyramids, Napoleon put the Mameluks, a dynasty of slave warriors who had controlled parts of the Ottoman Empire for seven centuries, to the sword. Twenty-nine French soldiers died and 260 were wounded; the Mameluk dead numbered in the thousands.

Napoleon's fleet remained a critical component of the Egyptian campaign because the ships provided an umbilical cord to Europe. Any food and supplies that the army might require would come by sea and the merchant and transport ships would need a safe place to unload. The entrance to Alexandria, however, was too shallow for large warships. The French commander, Vice-Admiral François-Paul Brueys, now in sole charge of the fleet, had no choice but to anchor in the majestic Aboukir Bay at the mouth of the Nile.

The unsuitability of Alexandria's harbour for a large fleet of warships is indicative of the poor naval planning that went into this expedition: Napoleon had chosen to invade Egypt without checking if the country's only harbour would shelter his fleet and by now the fleet was too weak to sail to Corfu, the nearest best alternative.

The water in Aboukir was shallow in places but offered good holding ground and an island at the southern end of the bay was quickly fortified to provide added defence, but the fleet was starving because the army had taken most of the supplies. 'We are floating between hope and despair', wrote Brueys to Napoleon.

Nelson finally found his prey in the early afternoon of 1 August when sailors scanning the horizon from the rigging of HMS *Zealous*, cruising ahead of the fleet, saw them in Aboukir Bay. The French saw the British at roughly the same time, from their anchorage. This moment was critically important: the French had not sent out their frigates to scout the water around Aboukir to provide warning of any potential attack but were simply basking in the Egyptian sun like lizards.

The fleets were even in number with thirteen ships of the line each, but the French were entirely unprepared for battle. Parties of sailors had been sent ashore to try to secure food and water and the ships' decks were still encumbered with civilian luggage and stores for the new colony. Most of the sailors who were aboard were poorly trained, unwell and hungry. The ships were not chained to each other nor were they anchored in the best possible location, close to shore. There was, indeed, a fatal weakness to their position. Each ship was at a single bow anchor, meaning that there was enough depth in a 360-degree arc around that anchor for the ship to ride in comfort. This meant that there was sufficient water in-shore of each French ship as well as to seaward, and the captain of the leading ship of Nelson's squadron, Thomas Foley of the *Goliath*, realized this.

Foley led his ship between the French fleet and the land, and was followed by six of his fellow captains. None of the French guns, facing the land, had been run out. Initially, the British opened an unreturned fire.

When Nelson reached the head of the French line in his flagship, HMS *Vanguard*, he sailed to seaward of the enemy and several of his captains followed his example. Now the French fleet was trapped between two fires.

Nelson's orders required his captains to anchor by the stern. This was an unusual and very difficult manoeuvre. Anchoring was a delicate and dangerous business for such enormous vessels and was usually conducted at a standstill. Now, however, with the ship sailing forward the largest anchor would suddenly be dropped from the stern in the hope that the anchor would bite and the anchor cable – as thick as a small tree for these largest ships – would hold. As the attack unfolded some ships succeeded and others failed. Those that failed found themselves heavily outnumbered and in serious danger.

The British ship *Bellerophon* was unable to halt her progress down the French line and ended up next to the French flagship, *L'Orient*, one of the largest French battleships of the period, with 120 guns mounted on three decks. Within an hour the *Bellerophon* was dismasted, on fire, her captain was unconscious, the first and second and fourth lieutenants wounded and her fifth dead. Her third lieutenant, Robert Cathcart, assumed command and at one stage was temporarily relieved on deck by a thirteen-year-old midshipman.

The battle had begun with the sun setting and by now the seascape was a blizzard of shadows. There were only a few sources of light. Flames licked out of the portholes of the ships that were on fire, and white, but dim, lanterns hung from the peaks of the mizzen masts of the British ships in an attempt to reduce the likelihood of friendly fire. The most significant light source was the guns themselves.

When they were loaded, a large cylindrical paper or flannel cartridge, full of gunpowder, was rammed down the barrel of the gun before the shot was inserted. The largest of these cartridges were more than 50cm long and 25cm in diameter. There were various types of shot. Cannonballs were fired at an enemy's hull while chain shot (two smaller balls attached to each other by chain) or bar shot (a small dumbbell) were used to target the enemy's rigging or personnel. The largest guns were on the lowest deck. On the British ships they were 32-pounders but some of the French had larger guns, 36-pounders.

The cartridge was essentially a self-contained bomb encased in the iron of the gun barrel. It was ignited by piercing the cartridge through a narrow hole in the gun barrel, pouring a small stream of powder into the hole and then igniting it with smouldering cord known as slow match or sparks from a flint. When the cartridge exploded the guns spat a bright tongue of fire as much as fifteen feet beyond the muzzle.

If you consider the number of guns at the Battle of the Nile the effect of this fire at night would have been extraordinary, a kaleidoscope of deadly fireworks that was unique to naval warfare. The British ships mounted 1,028 cannon, the French 1,098; a total of 2,126. Now consider that most famous land battle of the period, Waterloo: at that battle Napoleon had 252 guns, the allied British, Dutch and Prussians, just 156.

Admiral Brueys, already suffering from dysentery, fought with great courage in a lost cause. Early in the action he was wounded severely in the head and hand before almost being cut in two by a round shot, but he refused to be taken to the surgeon and remained on the quarterdeck. Other French captains fought like Brueys. Commodore Aristide Aubert Dupetit-Thouars of the *Tonnant* lost both arms and a leg but still encouraged his men as he died. In addition to Brueys, nine of the thirteen French captains died in the battle.

Nelson was also wounded. Roughly two hours into the battle he was struck on the head by a flying splinter which cut his forehead to the bone above his right eye, already blinded from a wound received four years earlier. The blood flow was appalling as it is with all scalp wounds, and Nelson thought he was going to die, declaring, 'I am killed; Remember me to my wife.'

Stitched up by the surgeon, however, it was soon clear that Nelson's time was yet to come. Although in great pain and probably severely concussed, upon hearing that one of the French battleships was on fire, he managed to get himself back on deck where he witnessed the culmination of his great victory.

The flagship *L'Orient* caught fire at about 10 p.m., possibly the result of British sailors from the *Alexander* using flammable grenades, a practice that was generally frowned upon. As she burned, a child was seen on the poop deck. This was the ten-year-old son of Commodore Luc-Julien-Joseph Casabianca; it is a scene that has been passed down through generations of children who know the first line of Felicia Hemans's poem 'Casabianca', which begins 'The boy stood on the burning deck'.

The scene was brief, however. The boy, like so many other sailors, threw himself into the sea to escape the inevitable explosion. The French ships immediately astern of *L'Orient* cut their cables and ran for safety and nearby British ships closed their gunports to protect their sailors.

Firing stopped in anticipation. When the explosion came every ship in the vicinity was damaged, the blast of light was seen nine miles away in Alexandria, and Commodore Casabianca's son was never seen again. British sailors picked up surviving Frenchmen in the water but fewer than 100 of her crew of 1,000 survived.

The battle then continued after dawn, lasted sporadically all day, and did not end until 3 August, when the French set fire to the *Timoléon*, which had run aground. At midday she exploded and the battle was over.

Nine British ships had either been totally or partially dismasted and three were put out of action, but only four French ships – two ships of the line and two frigates – escaped. Eleven French ships of the line had been either captured or destroyed, an unprecedented level of naval victory.

The ships of 8,930 Frenchmen had been destroyed or captured; 5,225 French sailors were either confirmed dead or had simply vanished in the tornado of battle; there were so many prisoners that the British simply could not cope and sent 3,105 ashore. In contrast, the British fleet lost a total of 218 dead and 677 wounded. Unsurprisingly, corpses, and parts of corpses, were washed ashore on the Egyptian coast for weeks after the battle.

Unusually for a naval battle, the strategic implication was both obvious and immediate. Nelson had simply removed the French army's link to Europe, its source of supplies and its means of escape. British naval power in the Mediterranean, which had been either entirely absent or pathetically weak since the alliance of France with Spain in 1797, was restored as a supremacy. Napoleon, his army and his colony, were stranded.

The recognition received by Nelson for his victory was unique in its international scope. Nelson was elevated to Baron Nelson of the Nile by King George III of England; Selim III, the Sultan of the Ottoman Empire, awarded him the Order of the Turkish Crescent; Paul I, the Tsar of Russia, showered him in gifts; and Ferdinand IV, the King of Naples, made him Duke of Bronté.

Nelson's more personal triumph, however, was that, upon arrival in Naples on his way home, he met Emma Hamilton, a remarkable woman and a famous beauty, and wife of the British envoy Sir William Hamilton. Such was Nelson's celebrity that Emma fainted when they met. Nelson then lived with the Hamiltons for several months and he and Emma fell deeply in love.

While Nelson lived the high life with the Hamiltons and basked in his celebrity, Fanny, his wife of eleven years, alone in rural Ipswich, faded from his thoughts.

In the aftermath of the Battle of the Pyramids, the Mameluks had retired to Syria, allowing Napoleon to consolidate his power uncontested. He did this with the appearance of friendship, tapping into the discord that had existed between the Mameluk ruling class and Egypt's Muslim population. Increasingly he associated his name with Mohammed in public spectacles; he was described as a 'favourite of Allah'; he became known as Ali Bonaparte and on several occasions wore oriental dress and a turban. His actual power, however, measured in healthy, loyal, numerous soldiers, had begun to run out like so many grains from an hourglass from the moment that his fleet had been destroyed at the Nile and his troops had been exposed to the desert heat.

The wheels of war moved slowly and in spite of the destruction of his fleet Napoleon's soldiers retained control of Egypt for three years. In that time Napoleon's army of architects, archaeologists and scientists got to work. Their most significant discovery was a large stone monument which bore an inscription of a decree passed by a council of priests in 196 BC during the reign of Ptolemy V. What made it so important was that the decree was written in three languages: Greek, Demotic Egyptian, and hieroglyphs. At the time hieroglyphs could not be decoded and no solution was discovered until 1820, but this monument, which became known as the Rosetta Stone, would provide the solution, utterly transforming our understanding of ancient Egypt.

The French remained in Egypt until 1801 but, frustrated with his progress there, Napoleon left for France in October 1799 and was lucky to make his way back without being intercepted by a British naval patrol. Then, in early November, encouraged by a faction of politicians, he seized power. The Directory was replaced by the French Consulate and Napoleon became the Consul. He wrote the laws of the new constitution himself and made certain that more power resided in his hands than in any other's.

This was the moment that the French Revolution ended and a dictatorship began. Napoleon, the soldier from Corsica, settled into his new rooms in the 230-year-old Royal Palace of the Tuileries, which had been home to five generations of French monarchs: Henry IV, Louis XIII, XIV, XV and XVI.

Thus the wheel had turned full circle around the axis of the Battle of the Nile. In 1794 the tyrant Robespierre had been brought down by men who feared power residing in the hands of one man, but now, in spite of the defeat at the Nile, Napoleon, who was as clever and as ruthless as Robespierre but with the added gifts of military genius, far-sightedness and limitless ambition, held that power in his hands.

The only way to stop him seemed to be at sea. Nelson's work was far from done.

Further Reading

Nicholas Blake *Steering to Glory: A Day in the Life of a Ship of the Line* (Chatham Publishing, 2005)

Sam Willis *In the Hour of Victory: The Royal Navy at War in the Age of Nelson* (Atlantic Books, 2013)

Roger Knight *The Pursuit of Victory: The Life and Achievement of Horatio Nelson* (Allen Lane, 2005)

Sam Willis *Fighting Ships, 1750–1850* (Quercus, 2007)